This Book Belongs To:

_____

_____

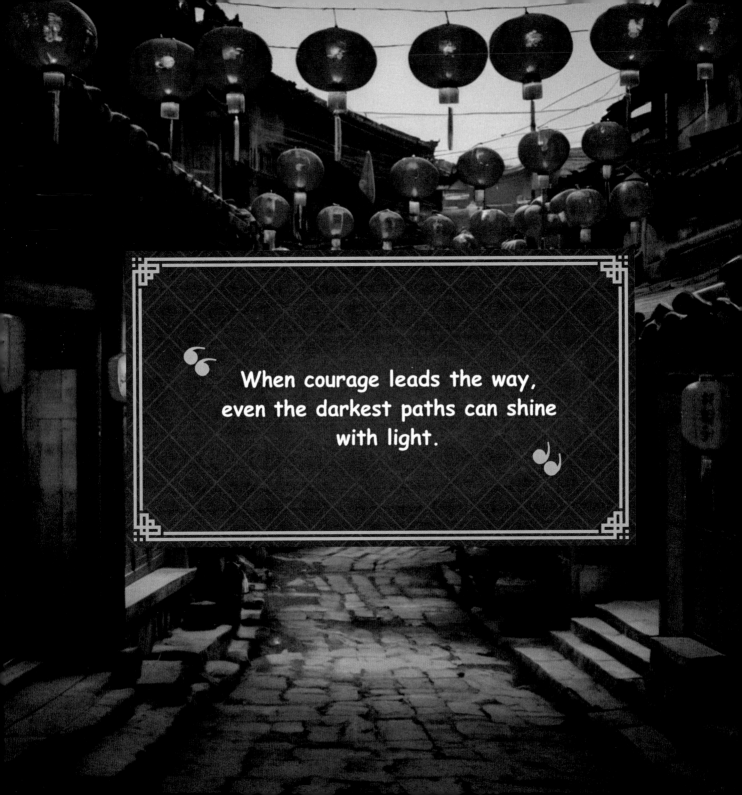

> When courage leads the way,
> even the darkest paths can shine
> with light.

Enter a world of magic and wonder as Mei embarks on a Lunar New Year journey like no other.

When a mysterious visitor arrives, Mei is whisked into an enchanted world filled with dazzling lanterns, hidden challenges, and ancient secrets.

With the fate of the New Year hanging in the balance, Mei must rely on her bravery and heart to overcome what lies ahead.

Will Mei unlock the magic needed to restore the joy of the Lunar New Year?

The Lunar Snake's Call

It is Lunar New Year's Eve, and the warm glow of red lanterns fills the streets of Mei's village.

Inside her home, the smell of dumplings and sweet rice cakes drifts through the air as her family laughs and prepares for the celebration.

Mei helps her grandmother hang the last lantern, her favorite one, shaped like a golden dragon.

Grandma smiles. "The lanterns guide good fortune and joy to us. But a long time ago, there was one lantern more powerful than all others—the Lantern of Light. It lit up the whole world and brought happiness to everyone. The Lantern was cared for by a magical snake, and without it, the new year couldn't begin."

"What happened to the snake?" Mei whispers.

"No one knows," Grandma replies. "But if the Lantern ever went out, someone brave would have to relight it."

That night, as Mei lies in bed, she stares at the shadows dancing on her ceiling. She can't stop thinking about Grandma's story. Suddenly, a soft hissing sound fills the room.

"Mei, I am **Suli**, the Lunar Snake"

She sits up quickly, her heart racing. A golden snake, glowing softly, coils on her windowsill. Its eyes shine like tiny flames.
The snake says,

"The Lantern of Light has gone dark, and the new year cannot begin. Without its light, joy and fortune will fade from the world. I need your help," says the snake, his golden scales shimmering.

"Me?" Mei whispers, trembling. "What can I do? I'm just a little girl."

"It's not your size, but your courage that matters," Suli says gently. "The Lantern's light can only be restored by someone brave and kind—that's you."

Mei hesitates. "What if I fail?"
"You won't be alone," Suli assures her. "Each step will make you stronger."

Mei takes a deep breath and nods. "Okay. I'll do it."
Suli's body begins to glow. "Then let us begin." With a flash of golden light, they disappear into the night.

The Lantern of Light needs three Flames of Fortune, each guarded by challenges. I will guide you.

With a flash of golden light, Suli whisks Mei into a magical world. The sky sparkles with stars, and everything shimmers in shades of red and gold.

-The Red Forest of Blessings-

"The first flame is here," Suli said softly, his golden scales shimmering as he coiled beside Mei. "But the fire rabbits are guarding it."

"Fire rabbits?" Mei blinked, confused.
From behind the trees, glowing rabbits leapt out, their fur shimmering like starlight and their eyes burning with playful fire. They circled Mei, giggling like bells.

"We'll give you the flame," one teased, twitching its ears, "if you play our game!"

With a burst of light, the flame shattered into glowing pieces, scattering through the forest. Some floated high into branches, others swirled on glowing breezes or hid in sparkling, shifting leaves.

Mei sprinted for the first piece, reaching for a branch, but it swayed out of her grasp. She jumped again—no luck.

"Focus, Mei!" Suli called. "You're faster and smarter than you think. Watch closely."

Taking a breath, Mei studied the tree's movements. She timed her jump perfectly this time, snatching the flame piece from the air.

Another piece floated lazily on the wind. Mei darted left, slid right, and finally leapt, catching it just before it escaped her reach.

As she turned, a rabbit appeared on a glowing stump, grinning. "This one's mine. Answer my riddle!"

A riddle?

I rise in the dark but burn with light. What am I?

Mei furrowed her brow, deep in thought. She glanced at the glowing pieces around her, her mind racing for the answer. Slowly, a smile spread across her face as the realization clicked.

She hesitated, then smiled. "A flame?"

The rabbit's ears shot up. "Correct!" It hopped aside, revealing another piece.

At a stream lined with glowing leaves, Mei hopped across quickly as they vanished beneath her feet.

The last piece hovered in the air. Mei grabbed it, and the fragments swirled together into a glowing flame.

"You did it!" the fire rabbits cheered.

Suli's golden eyes gleamed. "Well done, Mei. You trusted yourself."

Mei smiled, holding the warm, glowing flame as the rabbits vanished into the trees.

Next, Mei and Suli arrive at the Dumpling
Mountains. Steam rises from the ground
like clouds, and the second flame glows on
a high peak, guarded by a golden dragon.

-The Dumpling Mountains-

"To earn this flame,y ou must make the perfect dumpling."
the dragon's booming voice echoed through the steaming
mountains.

"Mei froze, her eyes widening as the golden dragon
descended from the peak. Its shimmering scales glowed
like molten gold, and its enormous wings stretched across
the sky. The ground rumbled beneath her feet as it
landed, its sharp eyes locking onto her.

"A d-dragon?" Mei stammered, her voice barely more than
a whisper. She had heard of dragons in Grandma's stories,
but seeing one—a real one—was completely different. It
was both terrifying and beautiful.

Suli, coiled calmly beside her, chuckled softly.
"Magnificent, isn't it?"

Mei swallowed hard, her heartbeat echoing in her ears.
The dragon's gaze softened just slightly.

Are you ready for the challenge?

Mei nodded hesitantly, her awe slowly giving way to determination. Her hands trembled slightly as she stepped closer. A small table appeared, shimmering in the golden light. On it rested a ball of soft dough, a bowl of fragrant filling, and a worn rolling pin.

She reached for the dough, her fingers brushing its soft surface, when suddenly the entire table beneath it began to quiver. A faint hum filled the air, and, to Mei's astonishment, the table lifted off the ground. Slowly, almost teasingly, it began to drift to the side, hovering a few inches above the floor.

"What?!" Mei exclaimed, her hands jerking back in surprise. She blinked, unsure if her eyes were playing tricks on her. But no, the table was definitely floating, the dough wobbling slightly on top as if mocking her.

Suli, perched nearby, tilted his head with a knowing smile. "Ah, the Enchanted Table. I was wondering when it would make its move."

"Why is this so hard?!" she huffed, holding up the misshapen dumpling for inspection.

The dragon's deep laugh rumbled through the air.

Perfection requires patience—and a steady hand.

Her first attempt was rushed, her hands trembling as she chased the drifting table. The result was a lumpy, uneven dumpling. Mei frowned, frustration bubbling up.

When the moment felt just right, Mei reached out and grabbed the dough firmly yet delicately. A sharp hiss of steam rose around her, momentarily blurring her vision, but she didn't falter.

Her hands moved with newfound focus, rolling the dough smoothly, adding just the right amount of filling, and pinching the edges closed with precision. Every movement felt deliberate, each fold crisp and even. Finally, she placed the completed dumpling on the table just as it began to drift away.

The dumpling gleamed softly in the dim light—perfect in every way. Mei allowed herself a small, triumphant smile.

The dragon's eyes lit up with approval—but it wasn't finished. Three more floating tables appeared, each surrounded by new challenges: swirling vines, gusting wind, and even tighter drifting patterns.

She nodded, wiping her hands and stepping forward, her determination burning brighter than her awe.

Through vines, gusts, and shifting steam, Mei worked —ducking, weaving, and timing her every move. Her hands moved with confidence now, folding each dumpling smoother and faster.

Finally, with a burst of effort, she placed the third perfect dumpling down. Panting, she looked up as the dragon smiled, its teeth glinting like gold.

"You have done well," it rumbled, opening its massive claw. The second flame hovered above it, glowing brilliantly.

Mei held out her hands, and the flame floated toward her, warm and alive. She smiled wide, clutching it close as Suli coiled proudly at her side.

"You faced your fear, and you mastered the challenge," the dragon said, its voice full of approval.

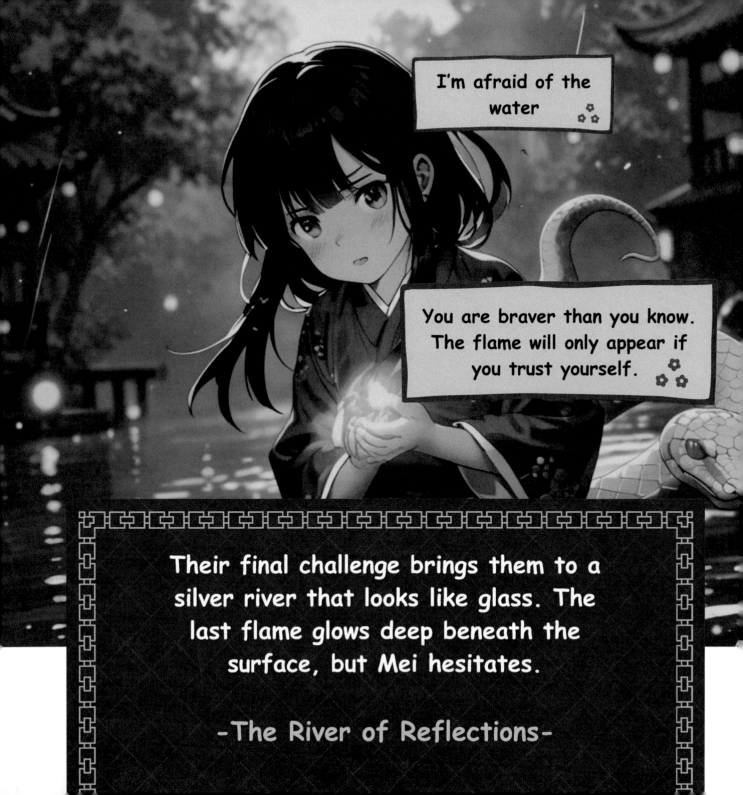

Their final challenge brings them to a silver river that looks like glass. The last flame glows deep beneath the surface, but Mei hesitates.

-The River of Reflections-

Mei stared at the river, its beauty masking its depths. Trust myself... She swallowed hard, then nodded, her resolve settling like a stone in her chest.

Taking a deep breath, she stepped into the water. It was cool against her skin, but not harsh. The ripples greeted her gently, like soft hands brushing against her legs. As she waded deeper, she caught sight of her reflection.

The face looking back at her wasn't frightened. Her reflection smiled—confident, calm. "You can do this," it seemed to say.

Her heart pounded in her chest, but the fear didn't hold her back anymore. With one last steady breath, Mei dove beneath the surface.

The world around her transformed. Shafts of silver light broke through the glassy water, illuminating the flame that hovered in the depths. Mei pushed herself forward, her arms outstretched, until her fingers closed around the glowing fire.

It flared to life in her hands, blazing brilliantly like a tiny sun, and for a moment, the entire river sparkled with light —golden and silver merging in perfect harmony.

Mei broke the surface, gasping for air, the flame still cradled safely in her palms. The water rippled around her, reflecting her triumph. She looked up to the sky, where the stars seemed to shine brighter, as if they too celebrated her success.

Suli's voice rang out softly, his tone filled with pride. "You did it, Mei. You trusted yourself. You've truly gathered all three Lanterns of Light."

Mei gazed at the flame, its warmth spreading through her, not just in her hands but deep in her heart. "It wasn't just me," she whispered, a smile tugging at her lips. "It was everything—the hope, the love, and the joy that guided me here."

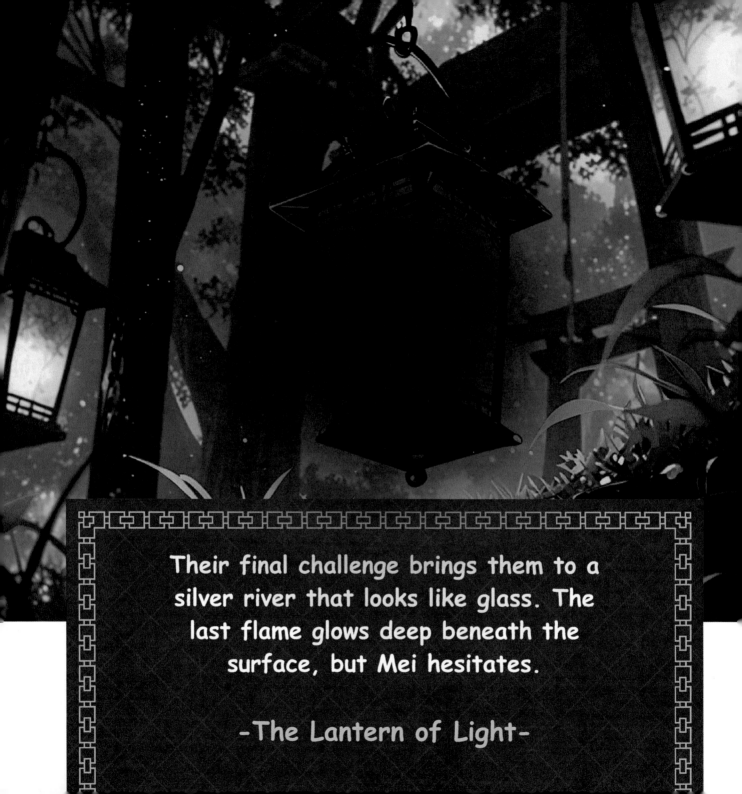

Their final challenge brings them to a silver river that looks like glass. The last flame glows deep beneath the surface, but Mei hesitates.

-The Lantern of Light-

With all three flames in hand, Mei and Suli made their way back to the Lantern of Light. It stood enormous in the center of the magical realm, its ancient form towering above them. But as Mei stepped closer, a chill ran through her. The Lantern was dark, its once-glorious light extinguished, and the air around it felt cold and still.

Mei carefully approached and placed the flames into the Lantern's receptacles, but... nothing happened.

A knot of panic tightened in her chest. "Why isn't it working?" she asked, her voice quivering.

Suli's golden eyes met hers, his voice soft yet firm. "You must believe, Mei. The Lantern's power comes from hope, joy, and love."

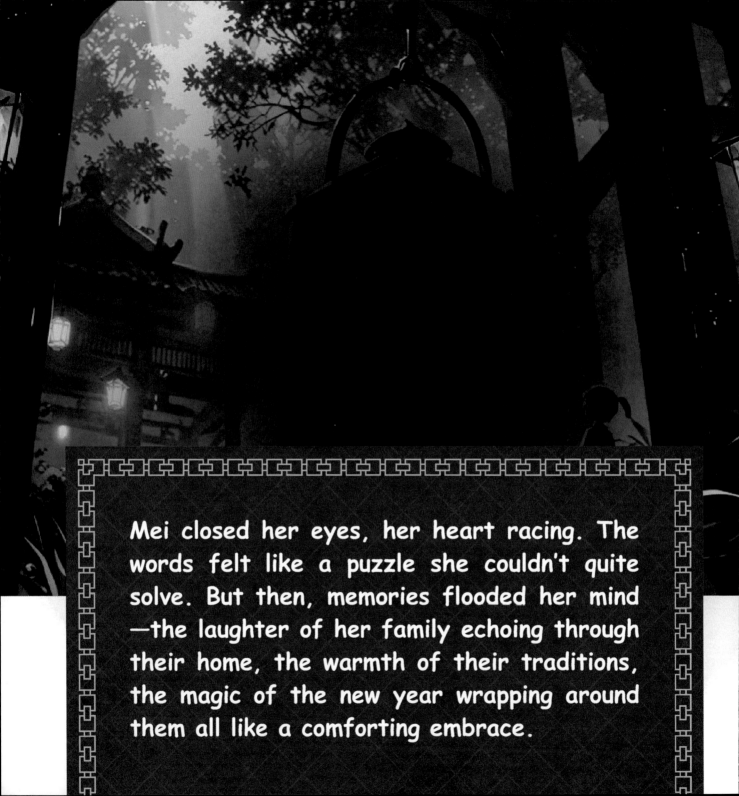

Mei closed her eyes, her heart racing. The words felt like a puzzle she couldn't quite solve. But then, memories flooded her mind —the laughter of her family echoing through their home, the warmth of their traditions, the magic of the new year wrapping around them all like a comforting embrace.

She thought of her grandmother's stories, the joy of sharing meals together, and the bright red lanterns that filled their home with light. She could feel her family's love, their togetherness, deep in her heart.

Taking a deep breath, Mei whispered, "Let the light guide us all."

For a long moment, nothing happened. Then, slowly, a brilliant light began to pulse from the Lantern. It flickered at first, then blazed to life, filling the sky with a golden glow. Fireworks erupted above, painting the heavens with brilliant bursts of color.

Mei's heart swelled with joy as the magical realm around her began to glow brighter and brighter, every corner filled with the warmth of hope and love.

Taking a deep breath, Mei whispered, "Let the light guide us all."

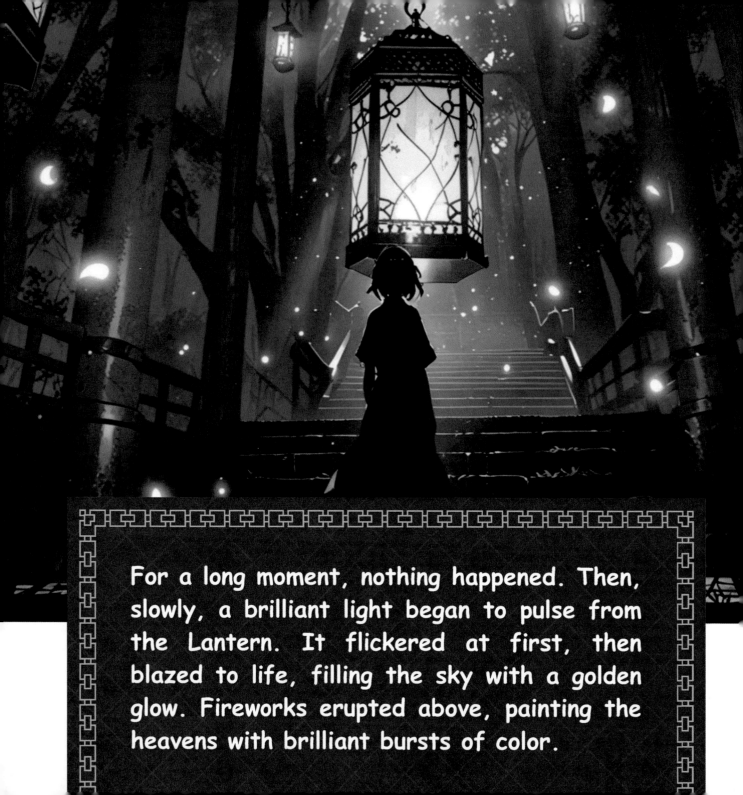

For a long moment, nothing happened. Then, slowly, a brilliant light began to pulse from the Lantern. It flickered at first, then blazed to life, filling the sky with a golden glow. Fireworks erupted above, painting the heavens with brilliant bursts of color.

Mei's heart swelled with joy as the magical realm around her began to glow brighter and brighter, every corner filled with the warmth of hope and love.

Suli's voice, rich with pride, echoed in the glow. "You have saved the new year, Mei. The world will never forget your courage."

In a flash, Mei found herself back in her bed. The warmth of her blankets surrounded her, and the sounds of the celebration downstairs drifted up to her room. On her pillow lay a small golden scale, a gift from Suli.

THE END

Anna Maplewood is a children's author who creates magical, heartwarming stories to inspire young minds. Her debut book, **A Mermaid's First Christmas,** and its sequel, **A Mermaid's First Jubilee**, form a delightful series celebrating friendship and wonder.

In her latest story, **The Lunar Snake's Call**, Anna continues to weave enchanting tales of bravery and magic, inspiring children to believe in themselves and the power of hope. Her books are crafted with care, aiming to spark joy and a lifelong love of reading in young hearts.

When she's not writing, Anna enjoys reading, cooking, and traveling to new places to gather fresh inspiration for her stories.

Wishing you joy, prosperity, and magical moments with loved ones. May your year ahead shine bright with courage and wonder.
— Anna Maplewood